To John, Matthew, and Kelsey
with love

The First ZOO

written by Henrietta D. Gambill

Third Printing, 1992
Library of Congress Catalog Card Number 88-63565
©1989. The STANDARD PUBLISHING Company, Cincinnati, Ohio
Division of STANDEX INTERNATIONAL Corporation. Printed in U.S.A.

A long, long time ago, God told Noah,
"Build an ark, Noah, build it big and
wide.
Because the animals are coming to
take a ride.

They will be coming, two by two,
and climbing aboard your floating zoo."

From places up high, came
big eagles and little bees,
and hooting owls from tall, green trees.

They came to the ark, two by two,
and climbed aboard Noah's floating zoo.

From places down low, came
scurrying ants and creeping snails,
and hardbacked turtles with wiggly
tails.

They came to the ark, two by two,
and climbed aboard Noah's floating zoo.

From faraway places, came
  long-necked giraffes and giant gorillas,
  and little, furry, gray chinchillas.

They came to the ark, two by two,
  and climbed aboard Noah's floating zoo.

From nearby places, came
purring cats and barking dogs,
and leaping frogs from hollow logs.

They came to the ark, two by two,
and climbed aboard Noah's floating zoo.

From dark places, came
flying bats and digging moles,
and quiet rabbits from their homes in
holes.

They came to the ark, two by two,
and climbed aboard Noah's floating zoo.

From light places, came
jumping kangaroos and gentle llamas,
and black and white zebras in striped
pajamas.

They came to the ark, two by two,
and climbed aboard Noah's floating zoo.

From hot places, came
    big-eared elephants and kudus with
    horns,
    but in all the animals, there were no
    unicorns!

They came to the ark, two by two,
    and climbed aboard Noah's floating zoo.

From cold places, came
long-toothed walrus and shiny seals,
and black and white penguins eating
their meals.

They came to the ark, two by two,
   and climbed aboard Noah's floating zoo.

From dry places, came
   kingly lions and humpbacked camels,
   and chattering monkeys, such funny
   mammals!

They came to the ark, two by two,
   and climbed aboard Noah's floating zoo.

From wet places, came
  slick, black sharks and giant, gray
  whales,
  and blue-finned fish with their own
  small sails.

They came to the ark, two by two,
and swam beside Noah's floating zoo.

This book has only some of the animals
God sent to the ark.

Can you think of others who came, two
  by two,
  and climbed aboard Noah's floating zoo?